WHAT FLAVOR IS YOUR BLISS

HOW TO FIND BLISS WITHOUT GIVING UP CHOCOLATE

DAVID FOGARTY

CONTENTS

What Flavor Is Your Bliss?

Print book layout and design: Aldilla Lara.

Ebook design and formatting: Steve Bremner

Published by Ahimsa In Action (AhimsaInAction.org) Berkeley, California USA.

ISBN: 979-8-9946787-1-8

All proceeds generated from this publication go to Ahimsa In Action, a non-profit tax exempt organization which promotes awareness of non-violence and public service in the United States and abroad through public education, and support for organizations and individuals with similar goals.

Want to share your experience with bliss or have a question. Please leave a comment at WhatFlavorIsYourBliss.com or email Dave at dave.whatflavorisyourbliss@gmail.com.

PREFACE

Experiencing bliss is the most loving, fulfilling and peaceful thing we can do. It explains who we are and our connections to other people, the earth and divine beings. This little book describes why you might want to seek your own bliss and provides some suggestions on how to get started. It's not a cookbook or a ten-step formula; bliss is a radically individual journey. My goal is to inspire you to get started on your adventure.

I don't have notable spiritual credentials other than the fact that I've walked the path toward bliss over many decades. It took a while, but I eventually found ways to experience bliss very deeply every day. On the journey, I learned about a few doorways to bliss that were helpful to me, and I humbly offer them for your consideration.

I've had many teachers on this journey starting with my parents who are our first gurus. But my education really accelerated when I met my teacher Jeffrey Armstrong whose Sanskrit name is Kavindra Rishi. Jeffrey provided the ideas and vocabulary to explain the bliss I had experienced as a young man. He is a scholar of Vedic philosophy, and a few years ago published a translation of the Bhagavad Gita —*The Bhagavad Gita Comes Alive*—which has been called "essential reading for all who want to understand the deeper truths of Vedic wisdom, the potential of eternal love, and the mysteries of existence."

Many of the ideas in my little book come directly from Jeffrey's teachings of the Gita and other Vedic texts. However, blame me for any mistakes in describing these ideas.

I've tried to keep the text accessible for those not familiar with some of the Sanskrit words and ideas you'll find here. There's a glossary and some simple explanations in the text itself. You don't have to accept these ideas as the truth, but I do urge you to think about them and figure out if they help explain your experience.

Safe Travels!

Dave Fogarty
December 2025

CHAPTER 1
WHAT FLAVOR IS YOUR BLISS?

Sometimes I forget that I was created for Joy.
My mind is too busy. My heart is too heavy
for me to remember that I have been called
to dance the sacred dance of life.
Hafiz

Footprints on the beach

People find bliss in countless ways—through love, prayer, music, nature, silence or service. My brother finds his by loving his wife, family and friends. My college roommate George found his by communicating with Jesus. Some folks sing. Yogis meditate. A Balinese priest uses energetic powers to find hers. My teacher Jeffrey connects with his by chanting the names of the Supreme Being. People find it by serving others. Billions of folks attend churches, synagogues, mosques and temples. Nature lovers find theirs by walking through the forest, splashing in the surf, or skipping rocks across a lake. And let's not forget those who find theirs with mushrooms or ayahuasca.

Experiencing bliss is the most satisfying, peaceful and loving thing we can do. Once we find it, we'll never want to let it go. I hope this little book will inspire you to search your heart and go to the center of your being to find your flavor of bliss.

WHAT IS BLISS?

When most people think of happiness, they think of everyday happiness, but bliss exists on an entirely different octave. We can't earn bliss, nor can we buy it. We can only receive it with gratitude. It's always here for us freely, abundantly and lovingly.

My first experience with bliss came when I stood on the Berkeley shoreline at sunset looking at the Golden Gate Bridge, the sand tickling my feet. I was 20-years old. I was not thinking about my university studies or my random love life. I wasn't looking for or expecting much of anything. And then it happened to me: I experienced being connected with the divine and the entirety of existence for that moment and for all time. This wasn't an abstract experience, and I wasn't on psychedelics. It was a potent feeling of personally belonging in a loving place where I danced with other souls and divine beings in this vast material universe, while at the same time being in a different dimension of eternal existence. I realized this was what I had been looking for a very long time. I didn't have these words at that moment to explain what was going on. I just stood there and experienced it. I saw it and tasted it. My mind was at ease, and this let me absorb what was happening without asking a million questions. It was something that I experienced at a deep level. I didn't know it then, but this was bliss. It's warm and cozy and loving, and it explains who we are and what we are a part of.

First, I wrote some very bad essays and even tried writing a short story attempting to describe the experience. None were published nor deserved to be. Gradually, the memory faded. It took me more than 40 years to rediscover the blissful experience and understand the treasure that I had been given. My odyssey to reclaim bliss started by studying Christianity, but that didn't feel like my path. I looked into other religions as well, but they weren't my way either. None of these explained my experience on that Berkeley beach.

Eventually I did find it. I not only rediscovered how to experience bliss, but I also now know bliss at a very deep level. I understand what it means, the doorways to enter so you can taste it, and the eternally satisfying experience of living in bliss every single day.

Your journey to bliss may take a few days or weeks on an easy and straight path. Mine was anything but that. I promise not to take you through all the twists, turns, dead-ends and false summits on my long journey. Instead, I will try to distill some of the key lessons I learned on my way toward bliss. Hopefully this will encourage you to take your own journey. You don't have to choose my path. As the first paragraph of this book described, there are many flavors of bliss. Bliss is radically individual and personal. The secret sauce is that we must desire it...very powerfully... and this will give us the will to take a walk toward bliss.

Perhaps you've already experienced bliss. Hopefully, this book will help you remember it. Here's what my friend Scott recalled after reading an early draft:

I have this very clear memory of when I was 10 years old. I cannot quite remember what stimulated the thought, but I remember thinking that I have had such a good life, and feel so connected to everything, and grateful, that if I died today, I would feel fulfilled. Strange thought for a 10-year-old to have. I was not under threat, I just felt happy and connected. Since then, I remember that experience all the time, especially when I feel like things are not going as great as they could, and it reinforces my gratitude and acceptance of bad things as just part of what has already been an extraordinary and fulfilling life.

Have you already experienced bliss? Do you have a memory of experiencing bliss in the past like my friend Scott? If so, please take a minute and write it down. If you'd like to share, do so at WhatFlavorIsYourBliss.com.

CHAPTER 2
MY NOT-SO-FORMULAIC GUIDE TO BLISS

I was created to smile to Love
To be lifted up. And to lift others up.
Hafiz

A friend once asked me if I had a formula for experiencing bliss. I don't. My personal journey has been more meandering than mapped out. There are no GPS coordinates for bliss—it's not on Google Maps. You can always Google "guru" and you'll find a long list of teachers, mystics, religions, wellness providers, self-help books and psychologists eager to offer their own version.

But here's the truth: This journey is deeply personal. There is no one-size-fits-all formula. We must find a path that's true to who we are and find teachers who resonate with that truth. How will you know when you've found bliss? You'll feel it in every part of your being. You'll know —not with your mind, but with something older, wiser and deeper. It will wrap you in love so complete you will feel threaded into the very fabric of the universe and the eternal world beyond time. In fact, that is who we really are. You will remember yourself, not as flesh but as essence—eternal, ecstatic and fully conscious. You'll know you're loved, fully conscious and connected in time and space—to the natural world, to other living beings, to the divine... and to the timeless essence of your own existence. That's our North Star. And it's always there to lead us home.

Even when I strayed far off course—even when I didn't know I *was* on a course—that feeling -- and a lot of help from some wise teachers helped guide me back.

Sorry, there's no ten-step formula, but what I can offer are five general tips that were doorways on my path to bliss. They're not commandments. Use what works, toss what doesn't. Create your own tips. Here are my five:

1. Say Thank You
2. Clean Yourself Up
3. Find a Teacher(s)
4. Figure Out Who You Really Are and What Your Mission Is
5. Consider Prayer

My journey appears so organized and systematic here on the written page, but it was pretty random. After all, my first brush with bliss came unexpectedly, standing on a beach in Berkeley, without even realizing that's what I was seeking. It took me 46 years to fully understand what that moment was about. Along the way, I've met others who've had similar awakenings. None of them ever forget.

Like Raymond, or as he prefers, "Earth Hippie." I met him one night camping at Walker Pass on the desert portion of the Pacific Crest Trail. He looked the part with a long ponytail, wearing a tie-dyed shirt and chain-smoking weed. Between hits on his bong, Earth Hippie told me the story of his life. During his stream-of-consciousness monologue, Earth Hippie revealed that he had been awakened when he was eight years old. By awakened, he meant what I now call bliss. Since then, he's known that he was an eternal being and always connected with the divine. He has lived from that knowing ever since. He follows the cues from his God, playfully navigating through this lifetime.

As far as I know, Earth Hippie never tried the following tips. And yet, he may be the most fully awakened and blissed out person I've met in this lifetime.

Raymond (Earth Hippie) and Dave at Walker Pass, California.

CHAPTER 3
SAY THANK YOU

My sister, Michelle

There's something about third-grade teachers. They are the happiest, nicest people on earth. Full disclosure: My sister, Michelle, is one of these angels.

Michelle's elementary school has a program to promote

values by focusing on a word every month. "Gratitude" was the word one month. Michelle taught the suggested curriculum lessons on gratitude, and they were effective. However, one afternoon, inspiration filled her as she walked over to a group of kids. "I'm grateful for you," she said to one of her students. The child beamed. "Wow, I'm onto something," she thought. She turned to the next kid and said: "I'm grateful for you." His face also filled with light. Michelle shared those magic words, "I'm grateful for you," with every student in the room. Michelle continued her gratitude lesson in class long after the values program ended. Gratitude is now an everyday part of her curriculum. Gratitude became second nature for the kids, spreading like the joy of catching a perfect wave.

One day the third graders entered the school library, turned to the librarian and said, "I'm grateful for you." The librarian was overwhelmed, and word quickly spread about Michelle's daily gratitude practice. The school's staff, from the principal to the janitor, came by to receive heartfelt gratitude from the children's pure hearts.

"I never expected that just saying this simple phrase, 'I am grateful for you,' would be so moving to people," Michelle said. "It's been like a giant wave of love expanding and growing outward from our classroom and into the community."

Every morning, third grade starts with sharing. Students raise their hand to tell what happened at home or on the playground. One little boy raised his hand to say that at dinner the night before he told his grandmother: "I'm grateful for you." Grandma cried with joy, and the whole family followed suit.

Who would guess that saying something as simple as "thank you" could be so powerful? Go ahead and experiment with expressing gratitude to the people and other beings in your life. Who would you like to say thank you to? Who do you appreciate?

Consider starting with yourself. You deserve kudos for the good stuff you do for yourself. One of my yoga teachers always tells her students to give ourselves a pat on the back for making it to class and getting on our mats. And don't forget to say thanks for all the little things you do during the day to keep yourself healthy. And for what you do for others, like taking time to call your mom or attend your kid's soccer game.

Saying thank you is more than just expressing gratitude. It's a way of confirming that you see someone. Even if it's perfunctory, it's still in the right direction, so make a point of saying thanks to your family, friends and neighbors, teachers, ancestors, and of course, your pets. Share gratitude with bigger beings like the earth, the sun, the moon and the deities who have touched and enriched your life.

Like those third graders, saying thank you every day changed my life. It's helped me to see the positive, even in challenging moments. It's deepened my connections—with people, with nature, with the unseen threads that tie us to something bigger.

And if you really want to master it?

In your next life, come back as a third-grade teacher.

CHAPTER 4
CLEAN YOURSELF UP

Untangle my feet from all that ensnares.
Free my soul. That we might Dance
and that our dancing might be contagious...
Hafiz

The next step on our journey is to clean ourselves up by removing the physical, emotional and spiritual gunk that clings to all of us.

I love Bali's water purification rituals known as *melukat*. Every day, Balinese people take part in this ritual, which involves being sprinkled with holy water, drinking it three times, and then washing three times. This cleansing has nothing to do with being soiled. It's to wash away the emotional, physical and spiritual gunk that gets stuck to us in daily life: the bitterness of a harsh word, the ache of betrayal, the unseen grime of anger, regret or shame. The Balinese know this truth deeply: to reach for bliss we must first be clean—not polished, not perfect, but getting rid of what no longer serves us, like rain washing away the debris from the road.

This isn't mysticism. It is practicality dressed in ritual. The Balinese accept what many of us resist: Spiritual and emotional debris accumulates, and if we don't clear it, this debris clouds our joy, dims our light, and poisons our peace.

The Balinese water cleanse is one way to clear the fog, to let go and soften the grip of what binds us. In the West, we often scoff at ritual. But I invite you to try it the Balinese way. Check out how to do it on WhatFlavorIsYourBlis s.com.

THE SOFT POWER OF FORGIVENESS

Forgiveness is another powerful soul cleanser. It's like taking a shower for the soul. But for the stubborn and proud among us, perhaps the two most difficult things to say can be: **"Please forgive me"** and its twin, **"I forgive you."**

Sages, avatars and many religions all champion forgiveness. It's one of the most powerful rituals ever performed to bring peace to ourselves and to the universe. Martin Luther King Jr. described it like this: *"Forgiveness is not an occasional act; it is a constant attitude."*

Forgiveness clears the debris that clouds our minds. It heals the hurt in our relationships. **We can forgive and be forgiven.** Forgiveness is a way of discarding the baggage so that we can move on to something far more soul satisfying: Giving and receiving kindness, compassion and unconditional love.

Forgiveness is like pouring clean water into a murky glass. Bit by bit, the water clears. The gunk—the grudges, anger and pain—dilutes. Forgiveness eliminates stress, fear and foreboding. It is a secret doorway toward bliss. The pure water of forgiveness eventually dilutes the grease and grime of human life. Here are a few specific actions that help:

- **Say a prayer** out loud that includes "please forgive me," asking the Supreme Being to forgive you for the wrongs you've committed.
- **Meditate silently and** forgive those who have hurt you and your loved ones.
- **Tell someone** who hurt you and your loved ones that you forgive them.
- **Meditate silently and ask for forgiveness** from someone that you've hurt.
- **Do a ritual cleanse** like the Balinese water purification ceremony.
- **Write down** what you want to be forgiven for on a piece of paper and throw it into the fire. (See Fire Purification blog at WhatFlavorIsYourBliss.com).
- **Make up your own ritual** to give and receive forgiveness.
- **Decide to forgive yourself,** which is sometimes the most challenging act of all.

We don't realize how much our grievances are harming us until we let them go. We all have a version of the "You Hurt Me List." The list makes us more resentful, angry, self-righteous and unhappy.

Building and keeping my "You Hurt Me List" was killing me. Thirty years ago, I decided to burn it. I needed to focus on helping my son Lucas and our family address his new diabetes diagnosis. The righteous grievances I was nursing were getting in the way of meeting that challenge, and so I just let them go.

I was done with resentment and the ugly shadows that got dragged along. I didn't use prayer, meditation or the above bullet points. If I had been practicing with these tools, I probably wouldn't have built up the grievances in the first place. I prepared for a long, involved process with perhaps therapy and other counseling; I didn't need it. I just turned on the tap of forgiveness and let its clean water begin to wash the dark stuff away. It was one of the best things that ever happened to me. I felt lighter and happier almost immediately. I treated my family and friends better. I started to enjoy life more.

Here's one more tip. A few years ago, my friend Hubert introduced me to the Hawaiian practice of *Ho'oponopono*, one of the simplest and most effective soul cleaners I've ever used. It was once used to heal rifts between families and is now shared widely as a personal practice of inner peace. It's four simple sentences:

I'm sorry.

Please forgive me.

Thank you.

I love you.

It really works, and I've come to rely on it to wash away the hurt feelings, anger and other negative emotions I cause for other people. I especially have come to rely on the *Ho'oponopono* with my wife of over 42 years. We know each other's wounds, where the bruises live, and like any long-married couple, we sometimes press them. I used to snap when triggered. Then I would defend and escalate. Now, I breathe and murmur the four simple phrases of *Ho'oponopono*.

If the wound is deeper, I approach the tough conversations in the spirit of *Ho'oponopono*. I'm still learning, using the trial-and-error method—my wife will attest to that—

but this simple ritual has lowered the volume in our home and raised the level of love.

CAN WE PRACTICE FORGIVENESS ABOUT SOMEONE WHO HAS DONE SOMETHING TRULY AWFUL?

I have lived a privileged life. I've only confronted a handful of truly terrible people, and only one who has tried to harm my loved ones or myself. If I'd been a soldier, a police officer, or a violent crime victim, forgiving would be so much harder.

I had an experience in Bali where I had to confront someone who was doing very despicable things to young people I love like family. I won't go into the details or name any names. It took some time for us to do so, but my wife Felicity and I faced up to the crimes we witnessed and took action to stop the behavior and heal our loved ones. It was a tough period for all involved. We helped some of the victims and those who were entangled in the guilt by association and the secrets they were forced to keep. However, we are uncertain whether we successfully changed this man's behavior or saved future victims. It's a lingering regret.

I've wrestled with the question for a few years: Should I forgive this man? I've circled around the question in several different ways. It's taken a few years and the anger has diminished, but I worry that forgetting what he did to those boys might allow the abuse to continue in the future. However, the more I've read about forgiveness, the more I'm convinced that it's the right course. This verse from the Bhagavad Gita goes straight to the point:

"Because you have free will, you can control your actions, but you are never in control of the fruit or ultimate outcome of what you do. Therefore, never let attachment to the fruits be the ultimate reason for your actions. Conversely, do not simply retreat into a state of detached inaction." (*The Bhagavad Gita Comes Alive*, Chapter 2, Verse 47)

I've also been reading Anne Lamott's ***Grace (Eventually)*** in which she quotes a friend: "You do what you can and then get out of the way because you're not the one who does the work. You're not in charge of the outcome, only the action."

Here's where I've ended up on this. I will love and forgive this man because my mission in this lifetime is to practice kindness, compassion and unconditional love. But I also plan to follow Krishna's and Anne Lamott's advice and not retreat into "a state of detached inaction." Rather, I will take further steps to stop the abuse if necessary and if I have the capability to do so, all the while remembering that I'm "not the one who does the work. I'm not in charge of the outcome, only the action."

My friend Scott points out that many Americans are facing a similar conundrum in how to deal with the darkness, death and cruelty caused by Donald Trump. He worries that the idea of loving and forgiving him may lead to doing nothing to stop his efforts to destroy our country. In fact, many people have adopted the strategy of not watching the news, so they won't feel dreadful. Others have decided not to join protests because they don't think it will make a difference.

My response: Take an hour to read about Mahatma Gandhi or watch the film *Gandhi* and you will see how one man committed to nonviolence can change the world for the better. The winning strategy, according to Gandhi:

"Whenever you are confronted with an opponent, conquer him with love."

I Need a Drink...of Water

I've focused on letting go of emotions, thoughts and other intangibles because for me these have been the most difficult attachments to remove. Of course, there are many attachments which can divert us from bliss. I mentioned a few in Chapter 2. These include thinking that accumulating stuff (cars, houses, fashion) will make us happy and blissful. It's seeking power, fame or a million other things. They just divert us from the path. Of course, we all need some stuff to survive as humans: a roof over our heads, food, etc. But when we begin to view these material desires as the goal of our lives, we will be very disappointed.

Let's go back to the metaphor of the glass of water. We start out life with a glass of water whose purity is determined by the choices we've made in our past lives. We can choose to clean up our glass, getting rid of attachments to everything but who we really are, or we can choose the other path and fill our glass with stuff that makes the water even darker. Cleaning ourselves up means removing our attachments to junk like anger, jealousy, greed and lust. If our container is cloudy, it's because we're focused on these desires. Instead, substitute this dark stuff with the purifying acts of forgiving and being forgiven...and let kindness, compassion and love flow in.

Kindness
Compassion
Love
Anger
Jealousy
Greed
Lust

CHAPTER 5
FIND A TEACHER(S)

The Do-it-Yourself (DIY) approach might have led me to rediscover bliss eventually, but it was taking a very long time. Finding teachers along the way helped speed things up for me. The trick of course is to find the teacher we need when we need them, and then ensuring they aren't fakes.

Not everyone is blessed with a mom who shares unconditional love. My Mom's love and the example she set started me on the right path. Without her, I would likely still be wandering around in the darkness. Our parents are our first teachers.

My growing love with Felicity. who has been my partner on this journey and my spouse since 1982. pushed me further on the rediscovery process. When I looked into my newborn sons' eyes I began to understand as well. I learned from friends, family, colleagues and even strangers. I learned it from doing service for others.

As you move forward on your path, you'll likely need additional teachers. For me this was a very random process because I didn't realize I was looking for bliss, but my intention to find it must have existed because I was guided to the teachers I needed at the time.

One of my early *gurus* was Ibu Gedong Oka. I met her when Felicity and I were traveling around the world with backpacks. We sent Mrs. Oka a letter asking if we could stay at her Gandhian *ashram* in Candi Dasa on the island of Bali. Frankly, I had no idea what an ashram was, but the cost appealed to me: $3 per night including meals. In 1980, we hopped on a bus stuffed inside and on top with Balinese villagers, chickens, pigs, veggies and fruit. It was a great way to get to know Balinese folks, but it was a hot and dirty trip. We heard the beautiful singing from the ashram temple when we got off the bus in the beach town of Candi Dasa. I fell in love with the place then and there as I listened to the ashram members singing their evening prayers.

Mrs. Oka was a diminutive but very no-nonsense woman. She was born in a small village in East Bali. She had moved swiftly up the social ranks, earning a university degree at Batavia University in Jakarta, a rare achievement for a woman then. Just before we met her, she had started her ashram at Candi Dasa on land her husband had bought as a beach house. The idea came to her after visiting India where she had toured Gandhi's Sevagram Ashram. Her mission was to help modernize her island by training young people in Gandhi's values, providing them with an education and sending them back into the community to become leaders. Later she became a member of the Indonesian Parliament and after her death she was honored as one of Indonesia's foremost female leaders with a commemorative postal stamp.

Ibu Gedong

Ibu Gedong and the ashram members welcomed us warmly and we joined in the routine of rising at 5 am for morning prayers, helping with chores and the garden, and returning to the temple at sunset for evening prayers. She taught us the values that govern a Gandhian Ashram, which are:

1. Ahimsa (Non-violence)

2. Satya (Truth)
3. Brahmacharya (Celibacy)
4. Asteya (Non-stealing)
5. Aparigraha (Non-possession)
6. Sharirik Khedu (Physical Labor)
7. Swadeshi (Self-reliance)
8. Sarvodaya (Welfare of All)
9. Nirmalata (Purity)
10. Seva (Service)

We also were immersed in Balinese culture, attending traditional ceremonies, visiting members' homes, and learning the language. Our intended short stay instead lasted six weeks. I'll never forget the blessing she gave us the night before we departed: *Jauh di mata. Dekat di ati.* (Far in eye. Near in heart).

I didn't know what a guru was all about, but it turned out that Ibu Gedong was a pivotal teacher on my journey. The *mantras* (prayers) we learned at the ashram stuck with us. Felicity and I regularly chanted them as we continued our backpacking adventure through Southeast Asia, India and Nepal. We continued reciting them when we returned to the United States. I also read Gandhi's works and practiced the values we learned from Ibu Gedong. We continued our relationship with her for several decades, and we passed down the mantras and our love of Bali to our sons Lucas and Max.

A vital practice we returned with from Ibu Gedong was this daily prayer ritual (*Pancha Semba*) which just about every Balinese person does at least once a day, sometimes more. It's five prayers that touch on our key relationships. The first prayer asks the Supreme Being to bless our *atma* (roughly translated as soul). For the second prayer, we hold a flower to our forehead and chant thank you to the sun, earth, moon and all the celestial beings. Third, also with a flower, is to say thank you to all the divine beings we already have relationships with or would like to be introduced to, and our teachers. Fourth, with flowers, is to ask for our friends and family to be blessed. And finally, the fifth, without a flower, is to ask *Bhagavan* (Supreme Being) to forgive our sins. And afterwards is *melukat*, the water blessing which I've described before, the purification ritual to help us eliminate the emotional and spiritual junk that accumulates in daily life.

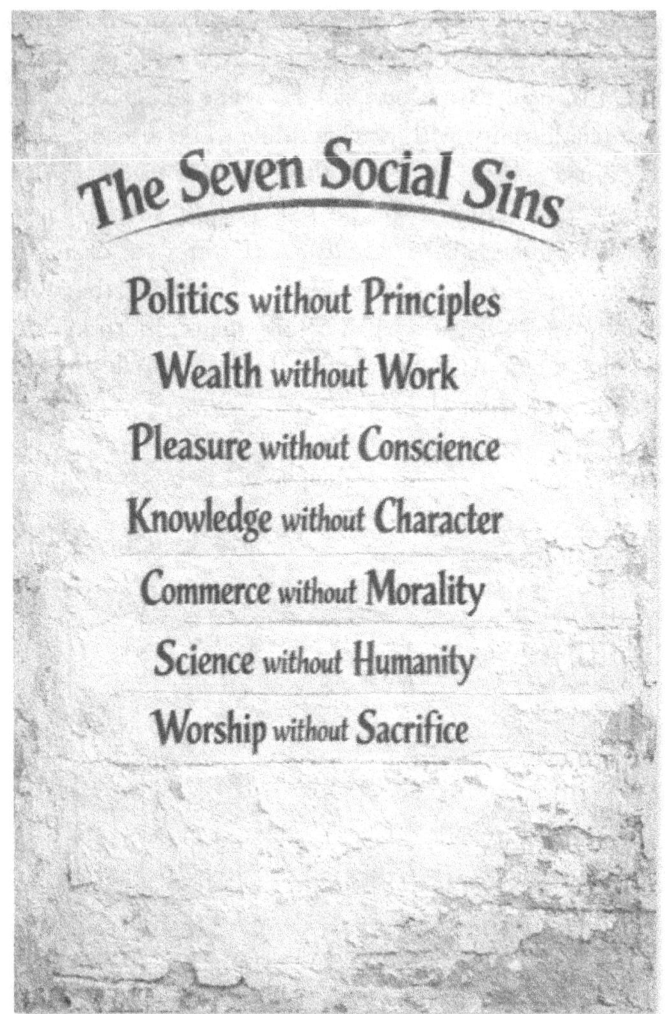

Gandhi's Seven Social Sins

At the time, I didn't fully grasp the meaning of these and the other mantras (prayers) I chanted, nor did I fully live the values we learned, but in hindsight my guru (teacher) Ibu Gedong guided me onto the path that eventually led me to bliss. I am eternally grateful to her.

Over the next 35 years I found additional gurus. Each teacher brought a unique lesson. Some came in flip-flops, others in suits, some in Jordans. A very important teacher was my longtime boss Dick Woodward who taught me about leadership and sticking to our values. Two of my best teachers were many years younger than I: My sons Lucas and Max. These fellas greatly deepened my capacity to love and serve, and I will always be grateful to them. Watching them grow and navigate their lives has been a profound educational experience. One of the big surprises of parenting for me was that at birth, these guys were fully formed atmas. I could glimpse their character right after they were born. They are quite different from one another, and it was vital for me to learn how to nourish them and support them on their unique journeys.

But what really revved up my journey was finding a teacher, Jeffrey Armstrong, who finally explained what those mantras I had been reciting for so many years really meant. He gave me the vocabulary and context to understand my experience on that day 46 years ago on the Berkeley shoreline.

Jefrey Armstrong (Kavindra Rishi)

I first met Jeffrey in 2016 at a yoga festival in Bali where a rainbow of people from around the world wore chic yoga togs, full-body tattoos, flowing robes and sarongs. Jeffrey sat on stage, clean-shaven, wearing khakis and a blue shirt.

He looked a little nerdy to be honest. I asked myself: Can a dweeby-looking guy with a WASPish name like Jeffrey Armstrong, not wearing any of the accoutrements of spirituality, really be one of the top experts in the world on Vedic philosophy? Believe me, he is that guy. He also goes by the name Kavindra Rishi.

Over the next year, I listened to many of Jeffrey's tapes and lectures. When I met him next, I asked how to know if a guru (teacher) is for real and not one of the numerous charlatans claiming guru status. He uses two criteria: 1) Does the guru walk the talk? Does he live his life in alignment with the values and ideas he teaches? After observing him for a couple of years, I can verify that Jeffrey lives what he teaches. 2) Does your guru's teaching come from a credible school of learning, and can he cite the source? For Jeffrey, this is the Vedic library which includes many, many texts such as the Bhagavad Gita, Rig Veda, the classic epic poems Ramayana and Mahabharata, and hundreds more. And, said Jeffrey, any true guru can provide the specific citation of the book, chapter and verse for the ideas he is teaching. I was a little skeptical about this remark, so I tested him several times. He instantly provided a reference for what he said. I looked it up and it checked out...every time. A teacher following the Christian way could do the same with the Bible as could an imam for the Koran, a Zen master for Buddhist texts, or a Jewish rabbi referring to the Torah.

I tried to read the Gita on my own many years ago, and it was just undecipherable mush. Although I understood that the mantras I had been chanting for decades were essential and were helping me, I didn't really understand their meaning. Jeffrey's teaching translated these for me so that I finally understood them. What seemed ridiculously complicated and foreign, he made clear. It was like discovering the Rosetta Stone.

The Gita's message is straightforward. Humans and other beings are eternal, individual atmas with the same qualities as Bhagavan, the Supreme Being who loves us unconditionally. We chose to come from our home in the transcendental realm—a place that is eternal and true, always conscious and inherently blissful -- to the temporary material world—the earth, planets and universes—to study and learn. It's our "Universe-ity," as Jeffrey would say. While in the material world, we experience many lifetimes in many different life forms, ultimately living in human bodies. In all of these temporary bodies we are subject to the laws of karma—cause and effect. After finishing our lessons in the material world, we return finally to the transcendental realm.

Chanting mantras helps us to remember all of this. Forgetting who we are and where we come from is a significant obstacle to finding our bliss. According to Jeffrey and the Vedas, chanting the names of the deities and the Supreme Being helps us remember who we are, but it's also a way of invoking deities, which allows us to begin building relationships with them.

It was a revelation to me that we can build loving friendships with the Supreme Being. It's not easy to get our head around the fact that the Supreme Being... who has a lot on his plate...is willing and very much desires to have a relationship with everyday people like us.

Short answer: Bhagavan (the Sanskrit word for the Supreme Being) loves us for exactly who we are. We share the same qualities. I know because I experience this love daily. We can't earn this love by good deeds or anything else.

It's just there for us when we're ready to experience it. All we must do is ask.

Jeffrey was the teacher I needed to open the doorway to conceptually understand what I had been experiencing. But I needed one more teacher to experience all of this at a deep, personal level.

My intention was not this clear when I decided to visit a holy man named Baba who lived in Coimbatore, India. Based on what I'd heard from others who had done this session, I understood that Baba provided the experience that was right for you. Fuzzy, I know, but I decided to go for it mainly because I trusted my friend and spiritual teacher Jana.

Jana had invited me to join her and Baba for a five-day intensive session for what she called SwaTantra training. I had previously studied with Jana and had learned some of the breathing and meditation techniques that were involved with the practice.

On the first morning, I did yoga and meditation with Jana, and then entered Baba's room. He asked me why I was here, and I answered with some kind of gibberish about wanting access to my energetic self. After some additional breathing exercises, he asked me to lie down. A few minutes later, the bliss started flowing. I saw Krishna (the Supreme Being in human form) sitting beside me. I felt that I was loved and fully connected in time and space with the natural world, other living beings and Bhagavan (Supreme Being). It felt the same as that experience on the Berkeley Beach 40 years before. Now I understand this experience better because I have the concepts to understand it, thanks to the Vedic teachings provided by Jeffrey.

I asked Baba what he had done, and he said, "I allowed you to experience what you wanted."

"But how do I repeat it?" I asked. "Just remember what you experienced, and it will return," he answered.

"But how do I experience it always?" I asked.

He said: "This has always been there for you, and always will be. All you must do is say yes to bliss."

Because of a family emergency, I was only able to spend two days instead of the full five-day session, but it didn't matter because the lesson I had come for was given to me that first time. I now knew that I had come to see Baba to rediscover bliss. That was apparently the goal all along. Baba could see that and showed me how to say: YES PLEASE!

My teacher Baba

I can't really explain exactly how Baba did what he did. My guess is that he's deeply empathetic and despite my own fuzzy intentions, he saw precisely what I desired and had the compassion and love to show me how to experience bliss again. Now that I've tasted the bliss, it's become easier and easier to access it. I don't really need to do the meditation or breathing exercises to taste the bliss. It's always there.

And that's how the answers to the questions that have been nagging at me slowly revealed themselves: *Who am I? Why am I here? Why would the Supreme Being care about me?* The answers weren't in a bolt of lightning or some booming voice from above. They came gently over time, in the form of teachers, mantras, books, babies, mothers, fathers, brothers, sisters, sons, bosses, a loving wife and Balinese friends who laughed when I mixed up the mantras. The answer was: *Because Bhagavan wants to be my friend. He wants to love me and receive my love in return.*

God—Divine Source, Creator, Brahman, Bhagavan, whatever name feels right to us—doesn't just care about us. We are made of the same stuff. We're not distant strangers. We are family. We've just forgotten. And the chants? The practices? The meditations? Our teachers left them as breadcrumbs to guide us on the path home.

I still forget sometimes. I still get caught in the noise of the world. But now, I know how to return. I close my eyes. I chant. I remember. And each time I do, bliss—*my* bliss—rushes in to greet me like an old friend.

When we wonder how to find our way, we should seek help from someone who reminds us of who we are.

Then say: **Yes, please.**

CHAPTER 6
FIGURE OUT WHO YOU REALLY ARE AND WHAT IS YOUR MISSION

Another key step to finding bliss is figuring out who we really are. Ironically, it was pondering the question of death that proved helpful in understanding who I really am, because when we ask what happens when we die, we're also asking who we are now, where we came from, what we're supposed to do in this life, and what happens when our biological body dies?

Before reading further, please take a moment to ask yourself those questions. If it's all a little murky, don't worry. That's where everyone starts. Figuring out who we are requires some curiosity and persistence. Are you a little bit curious about what you might find if you peeked inside, let go of how you've thought of yourself, dispensed with how others perceive you, and instead shone a bright light on your true self?

What do you see? Are we simply a bag of blood, skin and organs...our physical body? We are more than flesh and blood.

Are we merely our emotional selves? Do we feel happiness, sadness, anger, silliness, anxiety, joy, comfort, love...

and the thoughts or experiences that evoke them? We can experience all these emotions, but they are not who we truly are.

Are we our desires? Is who we really are defined by our desire for wealth, sex, food or power? We are more than this.

Look deeper still. Are we our thoughts? The mind is a wonderful tool, and it reportedly generates thousands of thoughts per day. Some of these are helpful, but many are just annoying and distracting. But it doesn't matter how many thoughts we have. We're something more.

Some believe we are *prana* or *chi*, which is the subtle energy that flows through our bodies and mental pathways. And that's true. But we're something more.

We too often define ourselves by how others perceive us. Are we loving parents and partners? Do teachers view us as smart, dumb or lazy? Do our friends consider us funny, loyal or assholes?

We are all of these: the physical body, mental body, intellectual body, subtle energy body, and we are influenced by our social ties with other humans, pets and other living things.

But does all that explain who we really are? It's interesting to understand that we are complicated and many-layered. But does it really get to the heart of the question for you?

These two wise guys do a good job of explaining what I'm trying to say:

"Your vision will become clear only when you can look into your own heart. Who looks outside, dreams; who looks inside, awakes."–Carl Jung

"At the center of your being you have the answer. You know who you are, and you know what you want."–Lao Tzu

I believe what Jung and Lao Tzu have stated here is true because I followed the path they describe. I invite you to follow your own path. Look into your own heart. Go to the center of your being. I can't give you the answer to who you are or exactly what path you should follow. This walk is yours to take, but it's well worth the journey to find out your true self, and then experience your own unique taste of chocolate...I mean bliss.

How will you know you've found yourself? You will know. It will feel authentic and true, and it will explain your experiences in this lifetime and the rest of them as well.

My journey took many twists and turns, but I eventually found my North Star by following what I now know is a conventional Vedic path. I found a teacher with a deep understanding of the Vedas who could explain it to me in words that I could understand. I've mentioned it before, but this is important so once again the basic idea: We are not our body, mind, emotions or thoughts. We are *atmas* who are eternal beings, fully conscious, joyous and individual. We come from the transcendental realm, which is permanent, eternal and where all consciousness exists, to the material world, which is the earth, the solar system and the universe, which is temporary. In the material world we live many lifetimes in human and other biological bodies. Our purpose for this journey is to experience this place and to learn. We are students. It's our university. The curriculum is our choice. After we learn the lessons that we came here for, we can choose to return to the transcendental realm.

All clear, right? I understand it's a lot to digest. Just sit with it for a day or a week or a lifetime and see if it helps explain who you really are. Maybe it will, maybe you will find different answers. A helpful tool might be to return to the questions raised at the beginning of this chapter:

- What happens when we die?
- Where do we come from?
- What's our mission in this life?
- What happens when our biological body dies?

This is a radically individual journey. You can choose to follow the teachings of Jesus, Buddha, Krishna or Mohammed. You don't really have to follow an established religion or philosophy. You can pursue a DIY curriculum like I have. I took a smorgasbord approach, eating from many different bowls of knowledge, choosing the bits that explained my experience before deciding that the Vedic diet of ideas and concepts is the most nourishing for me at this time. That may change because I still have much to learn about living as an atma.

Tantra practices also were an essential tool in figuring out who I am. (Sorry, this isn't tantra in the erotic way it's often depicted in the West.) Using tantra practices helped me feel, see and taste bliss very deeply and completely. Tantra practices are specific tools, sometimes guided meditations, yoga, and mantras that allow us to explore ourselves and our connection to the divine. It's the same tool that Baba used to help me taste bliss.

It took some time to understand what it means to live as an atma, my authentic self, defined as eternal, fully conscious, blissful and individual. My first step was seeing myself. Literally. I met a sage Balinese man named Ida Wayan Jelantek. He taught me a meditation that focuses on seeing oneself. I began by visualizing my liver and making it glow white. Then I visualized a white flower growing from my liver and saw myself dancing on that flower. In the final step, I moved my dancing self to right in front of me, and saw what a loving, joyous being I am. From the liver, I moved to my kidneys, gall bladder, heart and finally the crown of my head...seeing myself more clearly as I moved through the meditation.

I don't know how or why, but this visualization practice about my body parts helped me to perceive the unseen me at the center of it all...my atma. I performed this meditation regularly for five years and my atma became easier to see. When I returned to visit Ida Wayan Jelantek he pronounced me ready for the more advanced meditation where I did this visualization at eleven locations on my body.

Ida Wayan's meditation helped me to see myself, but just trying to be an eternal being day-to-day changed my perspective on many things, especially time. If we are eternal beings with many lifetimes to live, we have all the time we need to learn the lessons we came here for. This helped me to relax. I don't have to get everything done in one lifetime. I can take as long as I need. And that's good because I'm a slow learner.

I'll pause here a moment so that anyone who wishes can express their skepticism about how a couple of times now I've casually dropped the idea of reincarnation into this conversation. I too was doubtful about having multiple lifetimes. I came from a Christian background which taught we live just one human life and then either take the elevator up to Heaven or down to Hell. That seemed a little simplistic to me, and more importantly I realized that one lifetime wouldn't give me enough time to master the curriculum I was supposed to study. However, as I gained more experience living in the world, reincarnation just seemed to explain what I was observing better than other ideas.

Think about the film *Groundhog Day*. In the movie, Bill Murray starts out as a shallow, self-absorbed jerk. He then lives through the same day (or lifetime if we stretch the metaphor) many times. First, he indulges his desires for sex, thrills and mayhem but eventually figures out that what was really fulfilling for him was to be kind, caring and loving. In other words, he used his many lifetimes to get an education on how to become a better atma.

Understanding that we are eternal beings also means accepting that everyone else is on their own journey but at different grades and departments at the university. This has helped me to give space and time for my family and friends whom I've worried were making some major mistakes in their lives. I now know that like me, they have all the time and as many lifetimes as necessary to make all the mistakes and to take all the courses they need to complete their education.

What about my curriculum? Once I began seeing myself as an atma, an eternal being, then what was I supposed to learn? I asked my teacher Jeffrey that question and he gave me an equivocal answer that subtly told me to figure it out on my own. I thought about it for a long time and consulted Bhagavan in my daily prayer. There was nothing equivocal in his answer: Be kind, compassionate and love unconditionally.

KINDNESS

Kindness is easy to understand, even if it may be difficult to practice. Be kind to ourselves. Take care of our bodies. Be sympathetic and forgiving to ourselves when we make mistakes and try to learn from them. Be kind to others. Help people when we can. Be kind to other creatures and to Mother Earth.

COMPASSION

When I think of compassion, I envision a gentle Mexican man on the Arizona border helping a poor American boy.

Many decades ago, I was in Mazatlán, Mexico. I didn't have much money, but it was enough for a bus ticket back to the border. One night I was robbed of my last few pesos and needed to get creative. My solution? I hopped a freight train to Nogales on the Arizona border. I was a dirty, tired mess when I crossed through immigration into America with a basket carrying my sleeping bag and little else. On the American side, an older Mexican man approached me and wanted to shake my hand. I was a little suspicious but shook hands anyway. When I took my hand back, I discovered the gent had given me a quarter. He smiled, patted me on the back and wished me *buena suerte*.

In my experience poor people are the most generous when times are tough. A little money in my pocket helped me to buy some fruit and carrots to feed me while hitchhiking from Nogales to San Diego. But what really sustained me was the feeling that someone, a stranger, saw my plight, cared and took action to help. This man's act of charity resonates with me 40 years later. By receiving his compassion, I understood the value of giving compassion. There are no small or large acts of compassion. Every act of compassion is priceless.

The standard definition is simple. Compassion means seeing someone is suffering and taking action to help.

Jesus is all about compassion. He walked into a crowd, saw who was suffering and acted.

"You're blind," he said to men in the back row. He walked over and gave them sight.

"You're sick. I can heal you."

"You're hungry and thirsty. Bring me a couple of loaves of bread and water and we can feed you all and have some wine too."

Miracles dazzle, but what's behind them? It starts with love for others and a deep empathy for their burdens. Those feelings of love and empathy are really the key to understanding compassion. From there, it's a short bridge to action: doing what we can to heal the pain and suffering others are experiencing.

We may not have the power to give the kind of miracles that Jesus did, but being compassionate can be its own kind of miracle for both the giver and the receiver.

I've focused on individual acts of compassion here, but it can be even more powerful when acting together with other people. Those who have worked with their churches, synagogues, mosques or non-profit organizations to feed the hungry, heal the sick and house the homeless can attest to the big miracles that can be achieved.

UNCONDITIONAL LOVE

"Love is patient, love is kind. It does not envy, it does not boast, it is not proud. It does not dishonor others, it is not self-seeking, it is not easily angered, it keeps no record of wrongs. Love does not delight in evil but rejoices with the truth. It always protects, always trusts, always hopes, always perseveres." *1 Corinthians 13:4-7*

My first guru was my mother. She was all about unconditional love, the kind described by the quote above. She gave out bushels of it to me, my sibs, her grandkids, her family and friends, and those she barely knew. When my mother said she loved you she meant she saw you for who you are and threw her arms around you and loved you no matter what.

Receiving this kind of love was such a gift. It gave me buoyant confidence in being who I am. It gave me a safe haven. It made me feel peaceful.

She went to a Christian church from which she distilled a simple philosophy: God is Love. This quote expresses her view: "We know how much God loves us, and we have put our trust in his love. God is love, and all who live in love live in God, and God lives in them." *John 3:16*

This idea is also at the core of Vedic philosophy. In this case, the Supreme Being (Bhagavan) is loving and all pervasive and dwells in everyone and everything.

I have not always been my mother's best student. I admit to sometimes giving out puny love, not the bountiful no-holds-barred kind. Apologies. But I know how I'm supposed to love thanks to Mom, the Vedas and more recently, Jesus.

After a tiring, wet hike down from Pinchot Pass in the Sierra Nevada mountains, my friend George and I set up camp near the Woods Creek bridge in the glorious Kings Canyon. The sun made a surprise appearance, and I took the opportunity to dry my gear and catch some golden trout for dinner. After this feast, I found a granite bluff overlooking the forest for my evening yoga and meditation practice.

For Bhakti yogis like me, meditation aims to build relationships with the Supreme Being and others. My meditations are usually interesting. Krishna may arrive for a friendly chat, sometimes Saraswati plays a tune, Ganesha takes care of a problem on his cosmic Helpline, or I just sit quietly with my own atma. That evening a very bright wave of energy struck me right in the heart and radiated through my whole body. I literally glowed while completely at peace and ecstatically happy. This pulsing, radiant energy was pure Love. I could see, feel, touch and taste it.

And then Jesus, yes that Jesus, appeared just in front of

me in a seated, cross-legged position. He told me he was sending me energy waves of Unconditional Love. This gift answered my prayer to understand and practice Unconditional Love. After receiving this bounty, Jesus asked me if I'd like to send some of that Love energy back to him. I tried. At first what I sent was weak and intermittent, but gradually I improved. My biggest challenge, however, was staying focused. Often, I would lose the moment as my mind tried to distract me with lots of tedious questions and thoughts. Jesus told me I must practice sustaining the exchange of love. I asked if he was here as my tutor, and he agreed. In this lifetime, part of my curriculum is to not only have an intellectual understanding of Unconditional Love, but to practice it and feel its energy.

Over the next several days of meditation, Jesus returned to tutor me. I utilized a breathing exercise to help me reunite with the taste of Unconditional Love. I inhale to breathe in Love and exhale to share it.

This breathing exercise has helped me to remember how to access this ecstatic Unconditional Love and extend the feeling longer as I build up my love muscles. Sadly, I'm not living up to the goal of always remembering and never forgetting. That may take a while. It's also much easier to experience the ecstatic feeling of love than to practice it in my everyday interactions with people. I'm trying.

My tutor is patient with me and is always there to help when I remember to ask. I haven't always had such a close relationship with Jesus. While I grew up in the Christian religion, the churches I attended never really gave me a taste of him. The rituals, dogma and culture of religion never spoke to me. That changed when I was in my late teens and I began to pray. Prayer helped me to develop a more personal but still weak relationship with Jesus. Later, I studied texts like the Sermon on the Mount which helped me to intellectually understand his very revolutionary message of Love...often far different than what the church had to say about it. When I became a yogi, I began to experience this kind of ecstatic connection first with Saraswati and then with Krishna. But this was my first in-depth relationship with Jesus. I always thanked Jesus during my daily prayers but didn't really have an energetic attachment with him. Now I do, and I'm very grateful to call him my teacher.

CHAPTER 7
CONSIDER PRAYER

I stumbled onto my path with a Do-It-Yourself approach. This next part is a little embarrassing but here goes. When I first began conversations with God in my teens, I was praying for practical stuff. I asked for help on my algebra test, to make me a better football player, and for God to encourage that cute girl in my history class to go out with me.

Geez, that was embarrassing but honest. I was a shallow and immature lad offering shallow and immature prayers to God, but God was willing to meet me where I was. I didn't have to be spiritually awakened. I didn't have to be living cleanly. I didn't have to be nice, kind or compassionate. All I had to do was start the conversation. This was another secret doorway. God didn't always grant my wishes. I got an A in algebra, but my football career ended after high school, and that young woman was wise enough not to date me.

I recognize that some of you might be uncomfortable praying. My friend Scott feels that way. Because he didn't grow up saying prayers, he can't relate to the idea of a

Supreme Being, and he tunes out my *way or the highway* message from some Christian sects.

I get it. If you don't want to try prayer, I honor that. However, you don't have to dive into the deep end of prayer. You can dip your toe into the shallow end of the pool and see how it goes. How to start? You can talk to Jesus, God, Yahweh or the Supreme Being. Or you could begin your dialogue with something abstract and safe like the Universe. Talk to Mother Earth if you're close to nature. Just close your eyes and say quietly that you'd like to be their friend. You can ask your friend for help with a problem or support for a project. Maybe, like me, you start with the small stuff. Later you can ask for help with more important things like dealing with a bad disease or healing a relationship with a loved one. And when you become more sophisticated, you can ask for help understanding who you really are and what you should do with this lifetime.

As you grow even closer, you can ask for their name and ask to see them. And when you really get close you can say: "Thank you. How can I help you? How can I be of service?" That's when you'll know you are on the right path.

My dialogue with the divine started as a thin, intermittent stream, but as I began to pray more regularly these conversations became less shallow. I don't know if praying was why I was granted that moment of bliss on the beach in Berkeley at 20-years old, but after that epiphany, my spiritual life began to grow much deeper because now I knew what the flavor of bliss tasted like.

Why did the Supreme Being choose to have a relationship with me, just an everyday guy? Are we important enough to be their prayer partner? It turns out we are. According to the Vedas, the Supreme Being resides in our hearts and is just waiting for us to make the connection. Based on my own experience, we don't have to wander all over the world and study ancient texts, consult oracles, practice rituals... That's all a lot of fun, but not necessary. We just have to say: "Hi, I'd like to be your friend."

CHAPTER 8
HOW DO YOU GET STARTED?

WHAT IS BLISS FOR YOU?

Maybe you already know the answer or can glimpse a part of it. If so, spend some time sketching out the details of your experience. Write it down. Draw it. Sing it. Tell someone else about it. What does it taste like? Get to know the experience intimately. Does bliss come and go or is it with you always? Is there something that you do or think about or experience that helps spark the bliss? If so, keep doing that thing all the fricking time.

You also might try knocking on the five doorways I described earlier:

- Start by saying thank you to yourself and everyone else.
- Clean yourself up by practicing forgiveness or the Hawaiian practice of *Ho'oponopono.*
- Find a teacher. Look around for friends, family, therapists, pastors, imams and others who might guide you to your own path.

- Figure out who you really are, and perhaps start bringing kindness, compassion and unconditional love into your life.
- Begin a discussion/prayer with a higher power.

IS BLISS SOMETHING YOU REALLY WANT?

Maybe it's not for you. Perhaps you want to do something else before finding bliss. You get to decide for yourself. No one gets to tell you what to do about tasting your bliss. My guess is that once you've tasted it, you'll just keep wanting more and more. It's okay to be greedy about wanting bliss. It's better than chocolate because we can indulge our craving without any side effects except for happiness, love and connection.

What if you've done some truly terrible things in this life or a past lifetime? Are you still allowed to taste the bliss? According to the Vedas, yes! You'll have to work through the karma you've created by your past actions, but Bhagavan is still there for you as well.

Do you have to buy into all that I've shared with you? Absolutely not! You don't have to believe any of it, but I invite you to be open to the idea of bliss. Play with it and dance with it in your own way, and if you begin to experience bliss even in a small way, I invite you to go deeper.

It's not required, but it sure helps to have a teacher to help us understand what we're experiencing. Be on the lookout for teachers. You likely will be guided to those you need. Be careful to vet them because there are charlatans who will take advantage of you. Remember the two criteria for choosing a teacher: 1) Do they walk the talk? 2) Is their teaching grounded in a credible philosophy?

SO, YOU'RE EXPERIENCING YOUR BLISS, NOW WHAT?

Tasting our bliss is a huge step. We've been awakened, but how do we stay awake. For me, the most important step is to live the remainder of this life and future lives as an atma, which means I am an eternal being (*sat*) who is fully conscious (*chit*), joyous (*ananda*) and individual (*vigraha*). With help from Bhagavan, I also figured out what my mission is for this lifetime: to understand and practice being kind, compassionate, and to love unconditionally. A few years ago I decided that it was time for me to take the path toward *moksha*, which is the liberation of my atma from the cycle of repeated birth and death and karma, and to return to the transcendental world. Tasting bliss is a big step on that journey, and thanks to my human and spiritual teachers, I'm being guided on the choices I need to make to be eligible for *moksha*.

So, what is your next step? Maybe it's breathing. Maybe it's loving. Maybe it's just remembering that bliss is always waiting inside of us, like sunlight behind the clouds.

It can be as simple as choosing to experience bliss for a few minutes each day. Talk to your human and divine guides. Ask for help. Offer thanks. As my teacher Jeffrey says: "Always remember and never forget who you really are. Whatever helps you remember do that. What makes you forget, don't do that."

Bliss isn't a far-off summit. It's our own flavor of truth, love and joy—ready for us to taste, right here, right now...forever.

CHAPTER 9
BLISS GLOSSARY

Atma. This is who we really are according to Vedic philosophy—we are atmas encased in layers of matter. Our atmas are immortal, fully conscious, joyous and individual. We have the same qualities as the Supreme Being, Bhagavan, but of course on a much smaller scale. Our home is the eternal transcendental realm of Brahman, and we have chosen to come here to the temporary material world to experience it. During our time here, our atmas have many, many lifetimes living within physical bodies that are born and then die. Upon each death, our atmas are reincarnated into a new body, and this cycle of birth and death repeats itself until our atmas have completed the lessons we came here to learn. At that point, our atmas can choose to be released from the cycle of birth and death and return to the eternal transcendental realm.

Avatar: Avatars are the Supreme Being in human form. Krishna and Rama are two of the most famous avatars in the Vedas, with Krishna's visit described in the epic poem *Mahabharata* and Rama's in the *Ramayana*.

Bhagavan: In the Vedic tradition, Bhagavan is the Supreme Being.

Karma: When atmas are in the material world, their actions and decisions are subject to karma, the laws of cause and effect. The consequences of their actions and choices continue with them as they reincarnate until the time they no longer take actions that cause them to accrue karma—In other words, when they complete their experience and education in the material world. At that point, atmas can choose to return to the transcendental world of Brahman. For a deeper discussion of karma, read Jeffrey Armstrong's *Karma: The Ancient Science of Cause and Effect.*

Krishna: A famous avatar of the Supreme Being Bhagavan who arrived on earth about 7,500 years ago to teach humans some important lessons that they had forgotten. Krishna's story is told in the *Mahabharata*.

Mantras: Sanskrit prayers or chants that often are used to control and focus our minds and to remind us of the basic teachings of the Vedas. They are also chanted to praise, express gratitude and invoke deities.

Material world: The earth, the planets, all living bodies, the universe...where existence is temporary and unconscious. Atmas, who are by nature eternal and from the transcendental world of Brahman, choose to come to experience the material world and learn the lessons they need to learn. When they complete their education in the material world, they return to Brahman.

Moksha: The point at which an atma has stopped accruing karma, marking its graduation day or liberation from the material world. The atma is now finished with the cycle of repeated birth and death, and can choose to return to the transcendental realm of Brahman.

Reincarnation: The concept that the non-material

essence of a living being (atma) begins a new life in a different physical form or body after biological death. This cycle of repeated birth and death continues until the atma has experienced life in all the different bodies of the material realm and completed the lessons it came to the material world to learn, or as my guru Jeffrey Armstrong puts it, has completed the curriculum of the Universe-ity.

Tantra/tantric: Despite what you may have heard, Tantra is about more than just sex. Tantra is beyond philosophy and the mind. Classical Tantra teaches that the material world (your body, for example) and your divine consciousness (your atma) are inseparably united. That core concept means that practices such as meditation, ritual, visualization and others are doorways to help you experience your true self and your connection to other atmas and the Supreme Being.

Transcendental realm or Brahman: The eternal realm which is always shining and conscious and the realm of experience on which everything rests and from which everything has emerged. Unlike the material world where everything is temporary, the Brahman or transcendental realm is permanent and eternal.

Vedas: A vast and ancient library of cosmological, philosophical, scientific and other texts. including well known ones like the Bhagavad Gita. These books provide scientific knowledge for working with matter including ayurvedic texts for keeping the body healthy. They also explain our nature as atmas, the transcendental realm of Brahman, and our personal relationship with the Supreme Being, Bhagavan Shri Krishna.

CHAPTER 10
A FEW BOOKS THAT HELPED ME ON MY JOURNEY

The Bhagavad Gita Comes Alive: A Radical Translation by Jeffrey Armstrong (Kavindra Rishi). The Gita is India's most celebrated spiritual text. Set more than 7,500 years ago, it is an enthralling philosophical discussion between the Supreme Being (Bhagavan Shri Krishna) and his dear friend, the mighty warrior Arjuna. By exploring the text in a new way, Jeffrey reveals the Gita's main secret: the possibility of having a relationship with the Supreme Being, which helps us understand the deeper truths about the potential of eternal love and the mysteries of existence. *Available at gitacomesalive.com.*

Karma: The Ancient Science of Cause and Effect by Jeffrey Armstrong (Kavindra Rishi). The book explores reincarnation, the deeper mysteries of the soul and ways in which cause and effect control our lives. *Available at jeffreyarmstrong.com*

The Sermon on the Mount According to Vedanta. This book is based on a series of lectures by Swami Prabhavananda, the founder of the Vedanta Society of Southern California, about the Sermon on the Mount. It offers both the essence of Christ's teachings and the essence of Vedanta philosophy. For those who find a conflict between Christianity and Vedanta, this book is a must. For those, too, who have lukewarm regard for the spiritual teachings of Christianity, this book is a game-changer: "Blessed are the pure in heart, for they shall see God." *Available at vedantabookstore.com.*

The Tibetan Book of Living and Dying by Sogyal Rinpoche. For more than 30 years this book has been a foundation stone for those on the spiritual path. According to the Dalai Lama who wrote the forward: "In this timely book, Sogyal Rinpoche focuses on how to understand the true meaning of life, how to accept death and how to help the dying and the dead." *Available online and in some bookstores.*

ABOUT THE AUTHOR

Dave Fogarty is neither a high priest nor a famous spiritual guru. He's just a guy who took a very long walk toward what turned out to be bliss. It took a few decades, but he eventually found ways to experience bliss very deeply every day. On the journey, he discovered a few doorways to bliss that were helpful, and he humbly offers them here for your consideration.

Dave wants to share this because experiencing bliss is the most satisfying, peaceful and loving thing we can do.

Once we find it, we'll never want to let it go. He hopes this little book will inspire you to search your heart and go to the center of your being to find your flavor of bliss.

Want to share your experience with bliss or have a question. Please leave a comment at WhatFlavorIsYourBliss.com or email Dave at dave.whatflavorisyourbliss@gmail.com.

Published by Ahimsa In Action (ahimsainaction.org) a non-profit tax-exempt organization that promotes awareness of non-violence and public service in the United States and abroad through public education, and support for organizations and individuals with similar goals.

www.ingramcontent.com/pod-product-compliance
Lightning Source LLC
LaVergne TN
LVHW010837120826
845149LV00017B/1484

9798994678701